100 facts
Venom

100 facts
Venom

Steve Parker

Consultant: Camilla de la Bedoyere

Miles
Kelly

First published in 2011 by Miles Kelly Publishing Ltd
Harding's Barn, Bardfield End Green, Thaxted, Essex, CM6 3PX, UK

Copyright © Miles Kelly Publishing Ltd 2011

This edition printed 2012

2 4 6 8 10 9 7 5 3

Publishing Director Belinda Gallagher
Creative Director Jo Cowan
Editorial Director Rosie McGuire
Editor Claire Philip
Volume Designer Andrea Slane
Image Manager Liberty Newton
Indexer Eleanor Holme
Production Manager Elizabeth Collins
Reprographics Stephan Davis, Ian Paulyn
Assets Lorraine King

ISBN 978-1-84810-476-1

Printed in China

British Library Cataloguing-in-Publication Data
A catalogue record for this book is available from the British Library

ACKNOWLEDGEMENTS
The publishers would like to thank the following artists who have contributed to this book:
Julian Baker, Mike Foster (Maltings Partnership), Ian Jackson, Stuart Jackson-Carter
Cover artwork: Ian Jackson
All other artwork from the Miles Kelly Artwork Bank

The publishers would like to thank the following sources for the use of their photographs:
t = top, b = bottom, l = left, r = right, c = centre
Alamy 32 imagebroker **Ardea** 12(b) Jean Paul Ferrero
Australian Reptile Park (www.reptilepark.com.au) 46(t) **Corbis** 21(tl) David A. Northcott
FLPA 17(tr) Rene Krekels/Minden Pictures; 28(b) James Christensen/Minden Pictures; 33(t) Fred Bavendam/Minden Pictures;
33(b) Fred Bavendam/Minden Pictures; 35(t) R. Dirscherl; 39(t) Gerry Ellis/Minden Pictures **iStockphoto.com** 31(c) Laurie Knight
Movie Store Collection 23(c) Walt Disney Pictures, Pixar Animation Studios, Disney Enterprises/Movie Store Collection
Nature Picture Library 10–11 Ingo Arndt; 16 Lynn M. Stone; 34(b) Wild Wonders of Europe/Banfi; 42 David Fleetham;
43 Wild Wonders of Europe/Varesvu **NHPA** 6–7 Ken Griffiths; 10(bl), 26 & 46(c) Anthony Bannister; 13(br) Bruce Beehler;
19 Daniel Heuclin; 31(b) A.N.T. Photo Library **Oceanwideimages.com** 24–25 Gary Bell **Photolibrary.com** 9 Paulo de Oliveira;
22–23 Wolfgang Poelzer; 27(tr) Alastair MacEwen; 29(tr) Satoshi Kuribayashi; 36–37 Gary McVicker; 39(b) Gamma
Science Photo Library 18 Alan Sirulnikoff; 21(br) B. Boissonnet; 46 Louise Murray; 47(b) Volker Steger **Shutterstock** 2–3 Kletr;
12–13(border) Arena Creative; 12(panel: clockwise from top left) Pertusinas, picturepartners, Jens Ottoson; 14 Rich Carey;
16(c) photobar; 17(b) vblinov; 20(tr) Anton Harder, (tr) David Kelly, (br) Anobi; 23(bl) Anna segeren; 25(br) John A. Anderson;
26(bl) orionmystery@flickr; 31(t) Audrey Snider-Bell; 33(c) almond; 44 bernd.neeser; 46(b) markrhiggins

All other photographs are from:
Corel, digitalSTOCK, digitalvision, John Foxx, PhotoAlto, PhotoDisc, PhotoEssentials, PhotoPro, Stockbyte

Every effort has been made to acknowledge the source and copyright holder of each picture.
Miles Kelly Publishing apologises for any unintentional errors or omissions.

Made with paper from a sustainable forest

www.mileskelly.net   info@mileskelly.net

www.factsforprojects.com

Contents

Beware – venom!

1 Venom is the name given to toxic substances made by an animal's body, which can be injected into another creature (or person). A huge variety of animals have developed the use of deadly body chemicals – from tiny spiders to large lizards. The more we know about these incredible creatures and their lethal venoms, the more likely we are able to avoid harm and even save lives.

▶ Spiders inject their venom using sharp fangs. The Sydney funnel-web of Australia has one of the most toxic venoms to humans.

Why have venom?

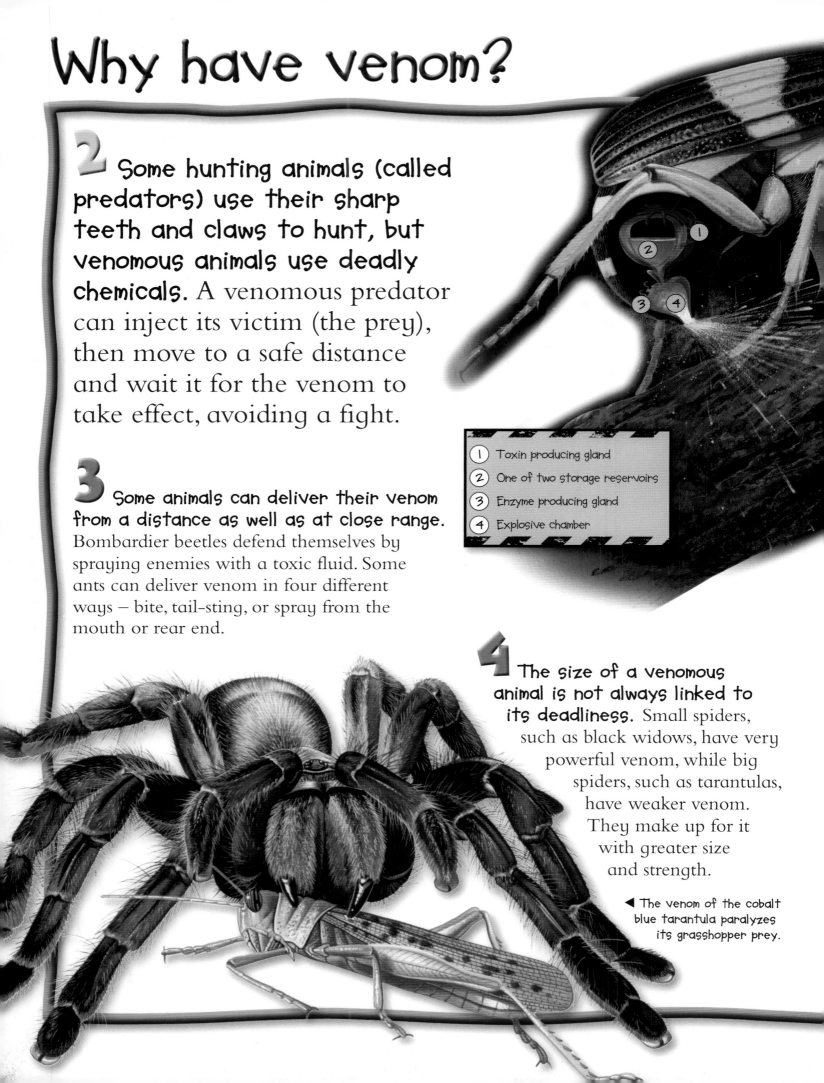

2 Some hunting animals (called predators) use their sharp teeth and claws to hunt, but venomous animals use deadly chemicals. A venomous predator can inject its victim (the prey), then move to a safe distance and wait it for the venom to take effect, avoiding a fight.

3 Some animals can deliver their venom from a distance as well as at close range. Bombardier beetles defend themselves by spraying enemies with a toxic fluid. Some ants can deliver venom in four different ways – bite, tail-sting, or spray from the mouth or rear end.

① Toxin producing gland
② One of two storage reservoirs
③ Enzyme producing gland
④ Explosive chamber

4 The size of a venomous animal is not always linked to its deadliness. Small spiders, such as black widows, have very powerful venom, while big spiders, such as tarantulas, have weaker venom. They make up for it with greater size and strength.

◀ The venom of the cobalt blue tarantula paralyzes its grasshopper prey.

◄ The bombardier beetle mixes two fluids, enzyme and venom, in its rear end. The explosive chemical reaction makes a nasty boiling spray used against attackers, such as army ants.

5 Venom can be used to protect against enemies in self-defence. Fish such as the lesser weeverfish, lizards like the gila monster, and insects such as wasps and bees strike out to protect against predators – they rarely use their venom to hunt. These animals often warn others of their deadliness by displaying bright, bold colours or patterns.

6 Venomous animals don't deliberately seek out humans to bite or sting. An attack usually happens in self-defence because the animal is surprised or feels threatened. Like most wild animals, venomous creatures prefer to avoid attacking large enemies.

Black dorsal fin is connected to venom glands

▼ Weeverfish live near the sandy sea floor, and often lie mostly buried with just their eyes, mouth and defensive fin spines showing.

9

Venom or poison?

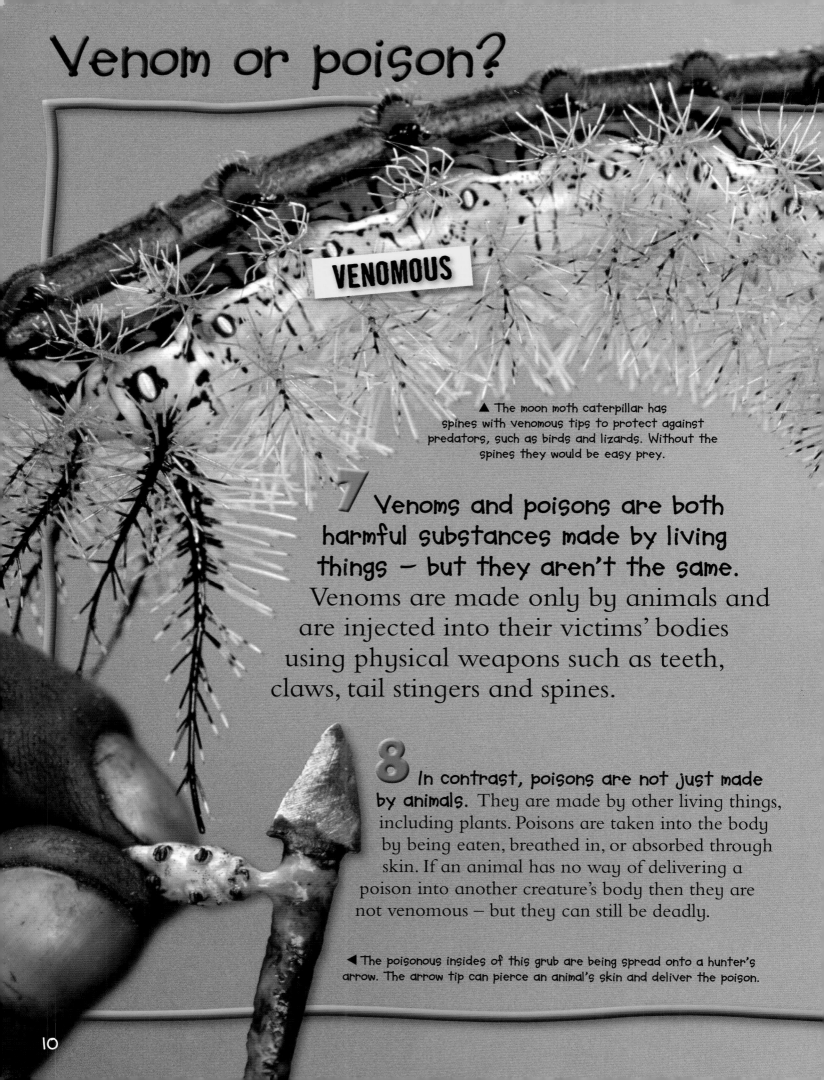

VENOMOUS

▲ The moon moth caterpillar has spines with venomous tips to protect against predators, such as birds and lizards. Without the spines they would be easy prey.

7 Venoms and poisons are both harmful substances made by living things – but they aren't the same. Venoms are made only by animals and are injected into their victims' bodies using physical weapons such as teeth, claws, tail stingers and spines.

8 In contrast, poisons are not just made by animals. They are made by other living things, including plants. Poisons are taken into the body by being eaten, breathed in, or absorbed through skin. If an animal has no way of delivering a poison into another creature's body then they are not venomous – but they can still be deadly.

◀ The poisonous insides of this grub are being spread onto a hunter's arrow. The arrow tip can pierce an animal's skin and deliver the poison.

QUIZ

Are the animals below venomous, poisonous or neither?
1. Lion 2. Rattlesnake
3. Black widow spider
4. Giant panda
5. Pufferfish 6. Rabbit

Answers:
Venomous: 2, 3 Poisonous: 5
Neither: 1, 4, 6

9 **Unlike poisons, many venoms may have little effect if they are eaten.** This is because venoms must mingle with blood and inner body fluids to do damage. If eaten, they are broken apart or digested in the stomach and are no longer harmful.

10 **The pufferfish is a poisonous, but not venomous, animal.** Its skin and some body parts contain a poison called 'tetrodotoxin'. Because the pufferfish has no way of delivering its poison, it isn't classed as venomous. The blue-ringed octopus, however, contains the same poison and *is* classed as venomous, because it has a sharp beak to bite the tetrodotoxin into attackers.

Spines to
inject venom

Protective spines erect when
fish inflates with water

11 **'Toxin' is the general name used for venoms, poisons and any other harmful substances made by living things.** Some microbes, such as germs like bacteria, can make toxins far more powerful than any venom.

◄► Porcupinefish are related to pufferfish, and some have poison in certain inner organs. Chefs are specially trained to prepare a pufferfish dish called *fugu* or *bok*. They have to learn which poisonous organs to remove.

POISONOUS

Potent poisons

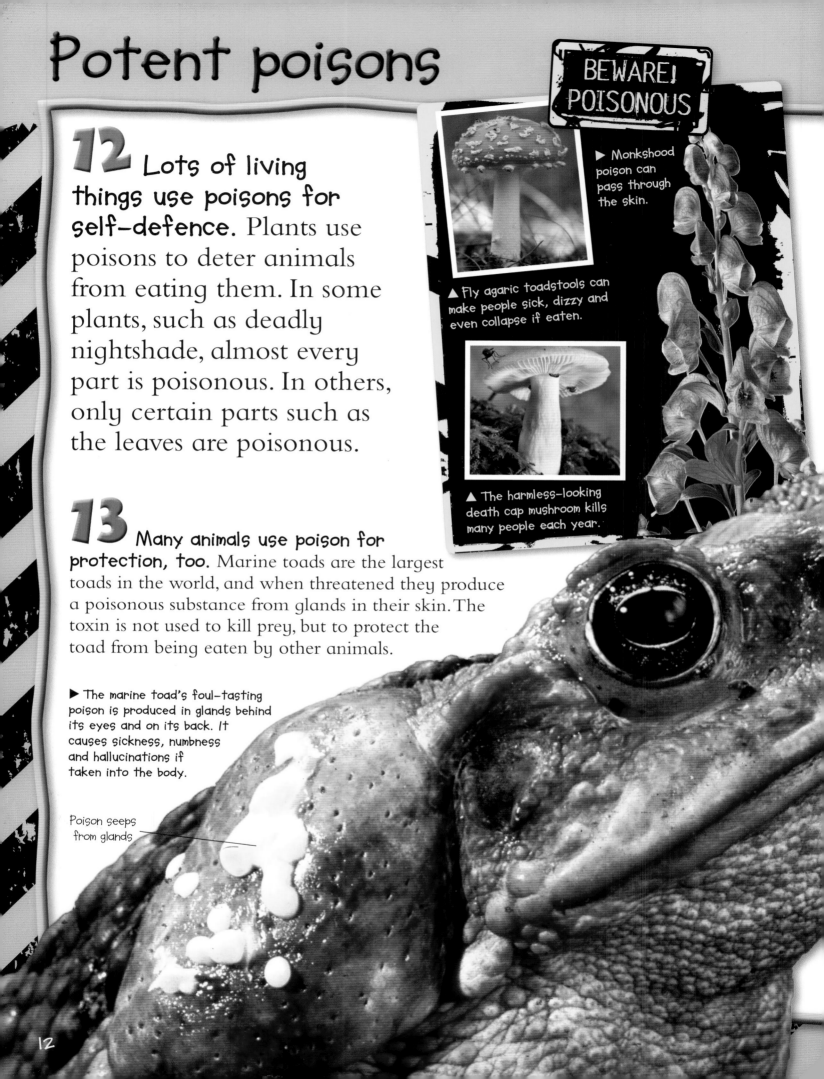

BEWARE! POISONOUS

12 Lots of living things use poisons for self-defence. Plants use poisons to deter animals from eating them. In some plants, such as deadly nightshade, almost every part is poisonous. In others, only certain parts such as the leaves are poisonous.

▶ Monkshood poison can pass through the skin.

▲ Fly agaric toadstools can make people sick, dizzy and even collapse if eaten.

▲ The harmless-looking death cap mushroom kills many people each year.

13 Many animals use poison for protection, too. Marine toads are the largest toads in the world, and when threatened they produce a poisonous substance from glands in their skin. The toxin is not used to kill prey, but to protect the toad from being eaten by other animals.

▶ The marine toad's foul-tasting poison is produced in glands behind its eyes and on its back. It causes sickness, numbness and hallucinations if taken into the body.

Poison seeps from glands

Poisonous skin

▲ The strawberry poison–dart frog's bright colours advertises its poisonous skin to possible attackers.

14 Some fish have horrible–tasting, poisonous flesh and skin. They include the pufferfish, cowfish, oilfish and jack. They are mostly slow-swimming fish – they have no need to race away and escape from predators, who avoid them.

15 Frogs, toads and salamanders are well known for the poisons that ooze from their skin. Small, colourful poison-dart frogs are the most dangerous – one type has poison that could kill dozens of people. Rainforest hunters wipe their arrows and blowpipe darts on its skin to poison the animals they shoot when hunting.

16 Very few birds or mammals are poisonous. Among the few are pitohui birds from Southeast Asia, which have skin and feathers that can cause numbness and tingling when touched, and sickness if people eat them.

▶ The blue-capped ifrita, a relative of pitohui birds, has a similar poison called 'batrachotoxin' in its feathers and skin.

Warning displays

17 Some venomous and poisonous animals display colours, sounds and other features. This is known as 'aposematism'. It allows other creatures to recognize them as potentially dangerous and avoid them. Young predators may try to attack venomous animals at first, but will soon learn from painful experience to stay away.

▶ Yellow and black are common warning colours, shown here on a fire salamander, which has poisonous skin.

▼ The lionfish's colourful, elaborate fins show that its dorsal (back) fin spines can jab in very powerful venom.

18 Bright colours and patterns are common signs that warn of venom or poison. Common examples are black with yellow or orange, as in wasps, bees, salamanders and gila monster lizards. Red and black occur in venomous redback spiders and horrible-tasting ladybirds.

Venomous dorsal spines

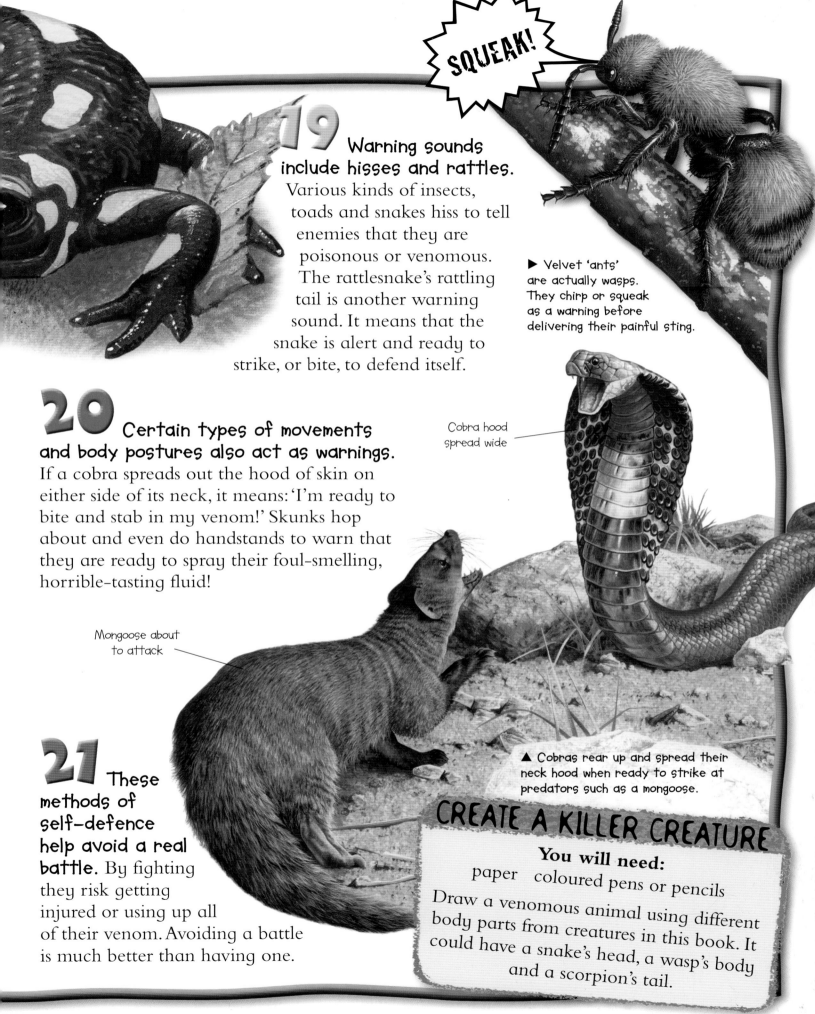

SQUEAK!

19 Warning sounds include hisses and rattles. Various kinds of insects, toads and snakes hiss to tell enemies that they are poisonous or venomous. The rattlesnake's rattling tail is another warning sound. It means that the snake is alert and ready to strike, or bite, to defend itself.

▶ Velvet 'ants' are actually wasps. They chirp or squeak as a warning before delivering their painful sting.

20 Certain types of movements and body postures also act as warnings. If a cobra spreads out the hood of skin on either side of its neck, it means: 'I'm ready to bite and stab in my venom!' Skunks hop about and even do handstands to warn that they are ready to spray their foul-smelling, horrible-tasting fluid!

Cobra hood spread wide

Mongoose about to attack

21 These methods of self-defence help avoid a real battle. By fighting they risk getting injured or using up all of their venom. Avoiding a battle is much better than having one.

▲ Cobras rear up and spread their neck hood when ready to strike at predators such as a mongoose.

CREATE A KILLER CREATURE

You will need:
paper   coloured pens or pencils

Draw a venomous animal using different body parts from creatures in this book. It could have a snake's head, a wasp's body and a scorpion's tail.

Venomous to who?

22 Many animals are venomous – but not to all other creatures, all of the time. Whether a creature can use its venom effectively depends on many things – especially on what kind of animal it chooses to bite or sting.

23 What people often mean by the term 'venomous' is whether the venom affects humans. For an animal to be considered venomous it needs to be able to puncture human skin. If it can, the venom needs to be powerful enough to do harm. If the animal can't achieve these things, it isn't venomous to us.

▼ The black widow spider is small but has sharp fangs stong enough to pierce human skin.

▲ The world's fastest snake, the black mamba, has venom so strong it can kill a human in 20 minutes.

24 How venomous an animal is depends on its health and strength. Also, if the animal strikes hard it is more dangerous than if it just gives a quick warning bite – some snakes will give attackers a quick jab, alerting them to their deadliness, but save the full impact of their venom for their prey.

25
Many people are terrified of house spiders. But small-to-medium ones can't pierce human skin. Really large house spiders can just about make a puncture, but they rarely do unless severely provoked. Still, their bite is rarely serious.

▶ The cellar spider looks slim and weak, but it catches and eats big house spiders. In humans its bite causes a burning feeling.

▶ There are several ways to measure venom strength.

26
Humans are quite big compared to most venomous animals and so often need be injected with lots of venom to cause real harm. A small caterpillar or fly, with thin skin, needs much less venom. The red-banded digger wasp has venom that easily paralyzes its caterpillar prey but the poison has no paralyzing effect on the human body.

TOXICITY RATING

☠ **CHEMICAL TESTS** These give the level or concentration of a harmful substance in a venom, such as calciseptine in black mamba venom, which attacks nerves.

☠ **BIOLOGICAL TESTS** Different amounts of venom are added to microscopic cells in glass tubes or flasks, to see how many cells are damaged or killed.

☠ **SPECTROMETRY** A venom is put through a machine called a mass spectrometer that shows which harmful substances it contains and how much of each.

▼ This red-banded sand wasp can easily pierce its prey's thin skin to inject paralyzing poison, but human skin is too tough.

Types of venom

27 Venoms are made in body parts called venom glands — but not all venoms are the same. Venomous animals contain various kinds of chemicals that affect different parts of their victims. Some animals can have several types of chemical in their venom.

Wasp

Sting

28 Many of the chemicals in venoms are substances called 'enzymes'. They alter the way living body tissues work. Each body part has thousands of life processes going on inside, which are controlled by enzymes. Venom contains different types of enzymes that interfere, causing the tissues to break apart.

29 Venom chemicals called 'neurotoxins' attack the nervous system. The nervous system is your body's control and communication system, made up of nerves and the brain. Venoms that attack it cause pain, paralysis, numbness and tingling. Neurotoxins can also affect breathing and heartbeat.

Swollen hand due to wasp sting

◀ Wasp sting venom has several toxins that disrupt blood flow, cause swelling and fluid to collect and produce severe pain.

VARIETY OF VENOMS

Type of venom	Effect on the body	Example animal
Myotoxin (proteolytic)	Leads to the breakdown of muscle tissue	Sea snake
Cardiotoxin	Causes cardiac arrest (heart failure)	Box jellyfish
Necrotoxin	The main effect is necrosis – the death of body tissues	Brown recluse spider
Haematoxin	Damages blood vessels and causes internal bleeding	Rattlesnakes
Neurotoxin	Severe damage to the nervous system	Blue-ringed octopus

30 Venom chemicals called 'haemotoxins' affect the blood and its circulation (flow) through blood vessels. They cause swelling and bleeding, and the blood may go sticky or clot, so it cannot flow to organs such as the brain. Because blood carries vital oxygen, clots can lead to shortness of breath and even suffocation.

31 Venom chemicals such as necrotoxins and proteolytic enzymes break apart body tissues into a mushy mess. Muscles go soggy and floppy, and skin turns into a goo. The lancehead snake has especially strong proteolytic enzymes.

I DON'T BELIEVE IT!

If certain kinds of strong-biting spiders were the same size as you, their sharp, deadly fangs would be bigger than bananas!

▶ Rattlesnakes have some of the most corrosive venom.

Delivering doses

32 Venomous animals have a wide range of weapons and body parts to deliver venom into their victims. Some animals such as the woolly bear caterpillars, starfish, sea urchins and fish use hairs or spines to break or puncture the skin.

HAIRS

▲ Thin, spiny hairs of woolly-bear caterpillars look soft but easily jab in venom.

33 Some venomous animals such as bees, wasps and scorpions have stingers at their tail end. The scorpion can use its fierce pincers and tail sting together. It raises its pincers and arches its tail over its head, ready to hold its victim and jab venom from above with its sharp tail tip.

▼ The spine tips of crown-of-thorns starfish easily break off, carrying their venom into the skin.

▶ The wasp's venom gland is near the sharp sting at the rear end.

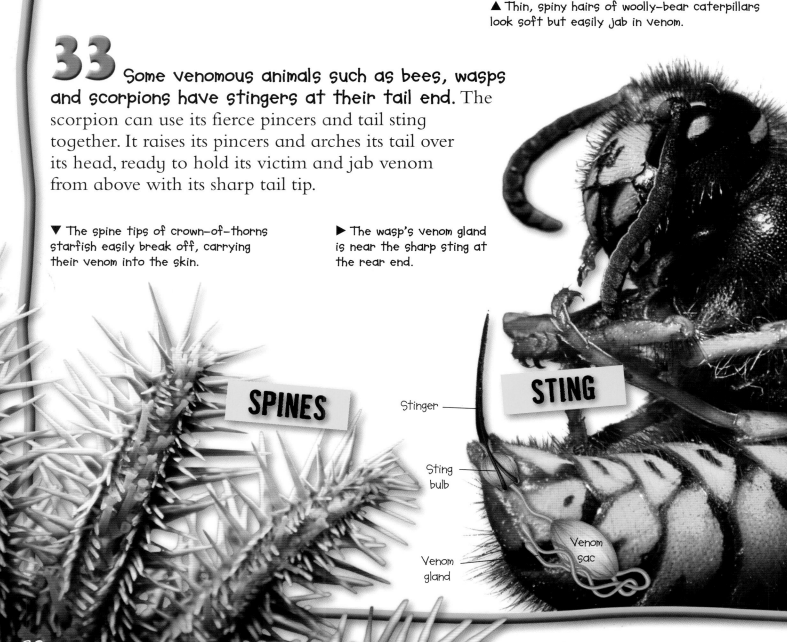

SPINES

STING

Stinger

Sting bulb

Venom gland

Venom sac

FANGS

Venom flows down hollow fangs

◄ The eyelash viper has especially long fangs that jab through the victim's skin into muscles, blood vessels and nerves.

34 **Most venom weapons are located in animal's head, near the mouth.** Venomous snakes have long teeth (fangs), connected to venom glands behind the eyes. The fangs are often grooved to allow venom to flow into a wound. Spiders also have sharp fangs to pierce their prey and centipedes have venomous front claws to deliver their poison.

▼ In some cases, venom pumps can be applied to bites and stings to remove toxic venom that hasn't gone too deep.

35 **If a person is bitten or stung by a venomous creature it's vital to get expert help fast, even if it does not hurt at first.** The quickest way is usually by calling emergency paramedics or doctors. Meanwhile the person should keep the bitten part lower than the rest of the body, and also stay still, so the venom does not spread around their body.

36 **If possible, the venomous animal should be identified, or described carefully to the medical experts.** Then they will know the best treatments to give, such as fast-acting medicines, and an anti-venom to work against that particular venom's effects.

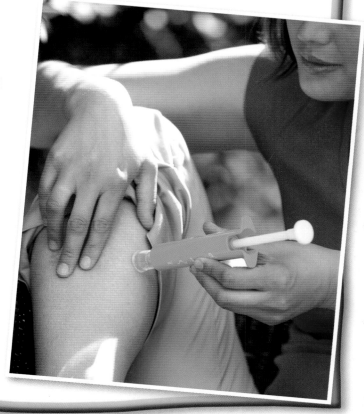

Jelly killers

37 Jellyfish don't look dangerous, but they can be deadly predators. They use stingers called cnidocytes (say 'nido-sites') to deliver venom. Jellyfish belong to the same animal group as sea anemones and coral creatures called polyps.

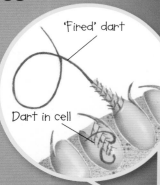

'Fired' dart

Dart in cell

► Cnidocytes keep their venom darts coiled up until touched, then fire them out to jab passing victims.

38 Cnidocytes are tiny harpoon-like darts that can only be seen under a microscope. There are hundreds or thousands of them on the tentacles of a jellyfish, anemone or coral polyp. When these micro-stingers rub against something they 'fire' by flicking out their sharp points to jab in venom. Clever boxer crabs have utilized the stinging power of anemones by grasping them in their claws and jabbing would-be predators.

▲ The Portuguese Man o' War's stinging tentacles dangle below the float and main body. They trail for up to 20 metres through the water.

QUIZ
Which of the animals listed below would a jellyfish catch and eat?
1. Baby fish 2. Blue whales
3. Woodlice 4. Sea-slugs
5. Shrimp 6. Earthworms

Answers:
1, 4 and 5

39 Jellyfish, anemones and coral polyps use stingers to paralyze their prey. The tentacles grasp their helpless victim, such as a fish, a shrimp or a worm, then slowly pull it into the mouth.

▼ In the movie *Finding Nemo* (2003), Dory the blue tang fish takes a while to realize that jellyfish can sting.

40 Some of the most venomous marine animals are found in the seas near Australia. The box jellyfish has extremely potent venom, as does the deadly Irukandji jellyfish, which despite its tiny size causes terrible burning pains, sweating, sickness and feelings of panic if stung.

▶ The Irukandji jellyfish's body is only the size of a small grape. The length of the tentacles can vary from a few centimetres up to one metre.

41 Fire corals are named after the burning pain caused by their stings. These small polyp-like creatures build beautiful coral shapes but should be avoided by divers. Sea anemones also have venomous stingers to catch prey, but only a few types are harmful to humans.

◀▶ Fire corals form yellow, green and brown branching growths.

23

42 **The mollusc animal group includes snails, slugs, squid and octopus.** There are venomous molluscs in the sea that can harm or even kill people. As with most venomous animals, this usually happens by accident – the creature bites or stings in self-defence.

43 **A coneshell is a type of sea snail, which jabs a small venom 'harpoon' into its victims.** The 'harpoon' is like a little barb or spear made of hard, stony minerals. It is on the end of the coneshell's proboscis, a bendy part like a tiny elephant's trunk. The beautiful colours and patterns of some coneshells attact people, who pick them up only to be stung.

▼ A coneshell 'sniffs' its prey with its breathing tube, then extends its proboscis (the snout-like body part) to jab the venom harpoon into a soft, vulnerable part of the victim's body.

Coneshell venom system

① The coneshell's deadly toxin is produced in the venom gland.

② Harpoon-shaped 'teeth' are stored in the harpoon sac, ready for use.

③ One venomous harpoon-shaped tooth is passed down the proboscis at a time (still connected to the venom gland) and stabbed into prey.

▼ The blue–ringed octopus can spit venom into the water to paralyze its prey or it can bite an enemy to stab in deadly venom.

...a fairly big blue–ringed octopus has a main body smaller than your fist. But it also has enough venom to kill more than 20 people within one hour!

44 Auger shells are another type of venomous snail. Although not as deadly as coneshells, they too have a harpoon-like barb on a bendy proboscis, which they jab into worms and other victims.

Blue-ringed octopus venom system

1. Salivary glands, where the venom is produced and stored
2. Sharp, hard beak, used to inject venom

45 The blue–ringed octopus is the most deadly mollusc. Its body is hardly the size of a tennis ball, but its venom is strong enough to kill a human. This small octopus lurks in rock pools. When it feels alarmed and ready to bite, it makes its rings glow bright blue as a warning.

46 Scientists have recently discovered that other kinds of octopus, cuttlefish and squid use venom. These molluscs bite their victims with sharp, beak-like mouthparts to inject venom when attacked. Like the blue-ringed octopus, the venom is in the animals' saliva (spit).

◄ This flamboyant cuttlefish changes colour in a flash to warn other animals of its venomous bite.

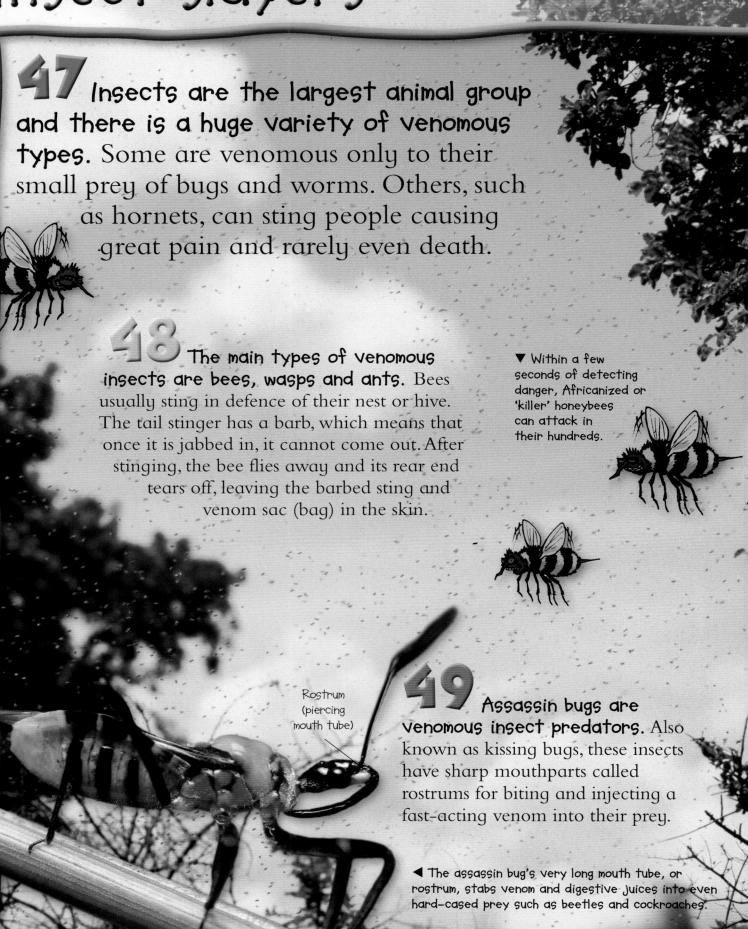

Insect slayers

47 **Insects are the largest animal group and there is a huge variety of venomous types.** Some are venomous only to their small prey of bugs and worms. Others, such as hornets, can sting people causing great pain and rarely even death.

48 **The main types of venomous insects are bees, wasps and ants.** Bees usually sting in defence of their nest or hive. The tail stinger has a barb, which means that once it is jabbed in, it cannot come out. After stinging, the bee flies away and its rear end tears off, leaving the barbed sting and venom sac (bag) in the skin.

▼ Within a few seconds of detecting danger, Africanized or 'killer' honeybees can attack in their hundreds.

Rostrum (piercing mouth tube)

49 **Assassin bugs are venomous insect predators.** Also known as kissing bugs, these insects have sharp mouthparts called rostrums for biting and injecting a fast-acting venom into their prey.

◄ The assassin bug's very long mouth tube, or rostrum, stabs venom and digestive juices into even hard-cased prey such as beetles and cockroaches.

50 Wasps have similar tail stingers to bees, but often the barb is small or missing and their stinger can be used several times. The wasp's sting is mainly for paralyzing or killing prey such as worms, caterpillars and bugs. It then takes its prey back to its young in their nest. Some even lay their eggs on the paralyzed victim, providing their young with food when they hatch.

▲ The Asian giant hornet has eight toxins in its tail-sting venom. But usually it tackles prey such as bees by cutting of their heads with its powerful mouthparts.

51 Ants attack their prey in two main ways. Some have proper stingers, while others bite with their sharp mouths and then spray venom from their rear end into the bite wound. Bullet ants are huge insects and their stings are said to be more painful than any other insect – up to 30 times worse than a wasp sting!

QUIZ

1. What are assassin bugs also known as?
2. Do bullet ants sting or bite venom into prey?
3. Which insect leaves behind a stinger after injecting venom?

Answer:
1. Kissing bugs
2. Sting 3. Bee

▲ Bullet ants grow to 3 centimetres long and sting small creatures such as spiders and bugs to take back to the nest.

Venom duct

Stinger

Dangerous spiders

52 **Spiders belong to the arachnid animal group.** They have eight legs and nearly all have venom for killing or disabling prey, or for use in self-defence.

53 **Most tarantula spiders aren't very venomous, so they use their size and strength to kill prey.** The fringed ornamental tarantula is popular as a pet, but its venom can cause great pain, paralysis, sickness and exhaustion.

QUIZ

Can you match up the spiders with the places they are from?
A. Sydney funnel-web
B. Southern black widow
C. Giant huntsman
D. Goliath bird-eater
1. North America
2. South America 3. Australia
4. Southeast Asia

Answer:
A.3 B.1 C.4 D.2

▼ The Brazilian wandering spider is so-called because it actively searches for prey. When attacking small animals, such as this poison-dart frog, it only needs to inject a tiny drop of its powerful venom.

54 How dangerous a spider is depends on many things. For example, if it is aggressive and ready to bite, or whether it prefers to run away and hide. If it does decide to bite, the venom is jabbed in by the spider's two fangs. Each fang is like a long, sharp, hollow claw on a base that contains the venom gland. The fang and base together are called the 'chelicera'.

◀ Spiders like this jumping spider make venom in the fleshy base or bulb of each fang. The spider's rear end is harmless and is used for spinning silk.

Fang connected to venom gland

Stomach

Spinnerets (silk glands)

55 One of the most aggressive spiders is the Sydney funnel-web. It is often found in and around houses and outbuildings in the area around Sydney, Australia. This spider will strike hard to inject its strong venom.

Two sharp fangs

▶ People used to die from the Sydney funnel-web's bite, but since an anti-venom was produced in the 1980s, far fewer people have been affected.

56 Black widows, Australian redbacks and New Zealand katipos can be overlooked because of their small size. But these spiders have venomous bites that can be deadly. The females have red warning markings on their black bodies and are more dangerous than the males, who are smaller and rarely bite.

Scorpions and centipedes

57 Nearly all kinds of scorpion have a venomous tail stinger. They stab toxins into their prey when hunting or during self-defence. When a scorpion is about to sting, it arches its tail over its back and raises the sharp tip, called the 'telson', above its head.

58 The emperor scorpion is one of the biggest types – it can grow up to 23 centimetres in length. But it is not deadly – its sting feels more like a bee sting. Smaller types, such as the dark-coloured fat-tailed scorpions and the pale death stalker from Africa and the Middle East, are much more dangerous.

Telson

Chela

▲ At 23 centimetres long, the emperor scorpion has the size and strength to overpower small prey such as mice and lizards.

◄ Scorpions use pincer-like claws, or 'chelae', to hold prey, such as this spider, as they jab in their tail sting.

▲ The giant tropical centipede grows over 30 centimetres in length. Pain from its bite lasts several days.

59 Most scorpions come out at night to hunt small creatures such as bugs, spiders and worms. By day they hide in dark places such as tree holes and under bark and rocks. But they can also wander near humans and hide in boots, drawers, cupboards and under beds.

▲ This centipede's head shows its two feelers or antennae. Below are the two curved, pointed poison claws, almost touching.

60 Centipedes are cousins of spiders and insects, but they have many more legs – and all are venomous. Their first pair of legs is specialized as long, sharp claws called forcipules, which look like pincers under the head. They are designed to stab prey and inject venom.

▶ Most centipedes, like this long-legged centipede, hunt small creatures at night.

61 Giant tropical centipedes such as *Scolopendra gigantea*, can cause great pain to humans. Luckily their bites are hardly ever deadly. Smaller kinds such as the yellow-legged centipede *Parotostigmus* have more powerful venom.

Stars and spines

62 Starfish and sea urchins belong to the 'echinoderm' animal group and are marine animals. There are several venomous kinds but they only use venom for defence – not to catch food.

63 The crown-of-thorns starfish is covered by fierce-looking spines. Each spine has an outer layer or sheath containing venom. If this jabs into human skin it causes great pain and feelings of sickness, which can last for more than a day. These starfish grow to over 50 centimetres across.

▼ Divers in the Indian and Pacific Oceans know never to touch the crown-of-thorns starfish. Its spines can even prick through gloves or wetsuits.

64 Sea urchins have long spines for protection, and also tiny stalked pincers for keeping themselves clean. Both of these can stab venom through human skin, even if touched very gently. The spine tips break easily and may get stuck in the skin, causing pain and swelling that can last for days.

Flower urchins of the Pacific and Indian Oceans have an especially nasty venom delivered by their waving mini-pincers on bendy stalks, called 'pedicellariae'.

65 Fire urchins have dangerous spines with enlarged tips that contain venom. This produces a stinging, throbbing feeling around the wound where the spines entered the skin. The diadema or needle-spined sea urchin has spine tips so thin you can't see where they end!

Fire urchins are flame-coloured and cause burning pain with their venomous spines, which continually move and wave on their ball-shaped bodies.

66 Sea cucumbers are also echinoderms. They have poisonous body parts called Cuverian organs, which they squirt from their rear end to defend themselves. If these parts touch a wound or sore in the skin, the poison can work like venom and cause numbness, tingling and pain.

The sea cucumber's favourite defence is to squirt out half-digested food, bodily waste, stringy slime, various poisonous body parts – or all of these!

Venomous fish

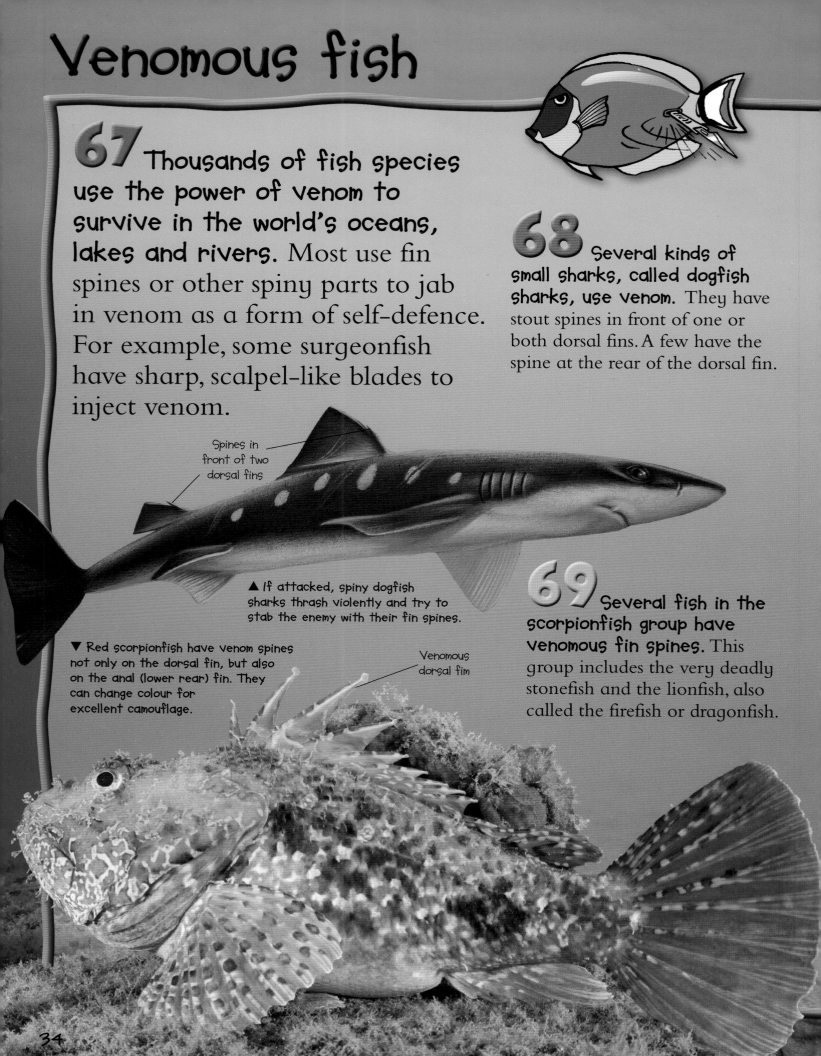

67 Thousands of fish species use the power of venom to survive in the world's oceans, lakes and rivers. Most use fin spines or other spiny parts to jab in venom as a form of self-defence. For example, some surgeonfish have sharp, scalpel-like blades to inject venom.

68 Several kinds of small sharks, called dogfish sharks, use venom. They have stout spines in front of one or both dorsal fins. A few have the spine at the rear of the dorsal fin.

Spines in front of two dorsal fins

▲ If attacked, spiny dogfish sharks thrash violently and try to stab the enemy with their fin spines.

69 Several fish in the scorpionfish group have venomous fin spines. This group includes the very deadly stonefish and the lionfish, also called the firefish or dragonfish.

▼ Red scorpionfish have venom spines not only on the dorsal fin, but also on the anal (lower rear) fin. They can change colour for excellent camouflage.

Venomous dorsal fin

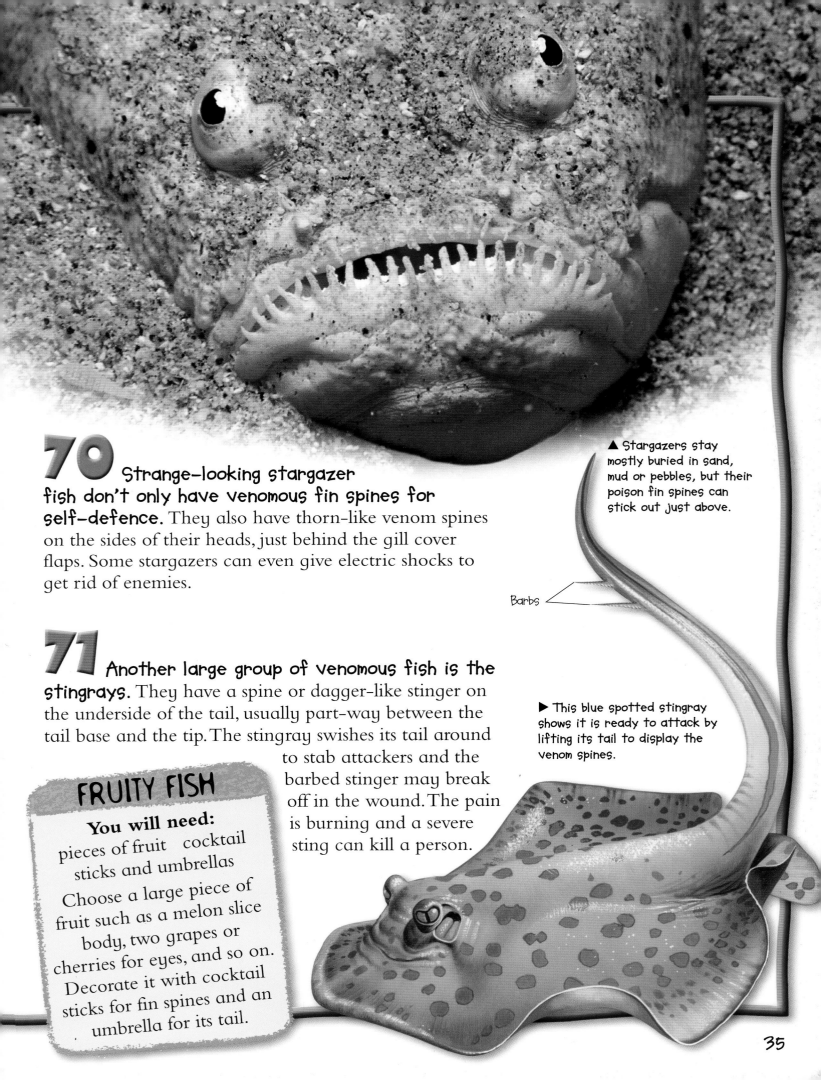

70 Strange-looking stargazer fish don't only have venomous fin spines for self-defence. They also have thorn-like venom spines on the sides of their heads, just behind the gill cover flaps. Some stargazers can even give electric shocks to get rid of enemies.

▲ Stargazers stay mostly buried in sand, mud or pebbles, but their poison fin spines can stick out just above.

Barbs

71 Another large group of venomous fish is the stingrays. They have a spine or dagger-like stinger on the underside of the tail, usually part-way between the tail base and the tip. The stingray swishes its tail around to stab attackers and the barbed stinger may break off in the wound. The pain is burning and a severe sting can kill a person.

▶ This blue spotted stingray shows it is ready to attack by lifting its tail to display the venom spines.

FRUITY FISH

You will need:
pieces of fruit   cocktail sticks and umbrellas

Choose a large piece of fruit such as a melon slice body, two grapes or cherries for eyes, and so on. Decorate it with cocktail sticks for fin spines and an umbrella for its tail.

Snake strike!

◀ Before a rattlesnake strikes, it shakes its tail rattle. It also lifts up and coils the front part of its body to get a good view of its victim.

72 About 600 species of snake have venom. They use it to catch prey and also for self-defence. Fewer than 100 kinds of snake can cause serious injury or death to humans.

73 Snake venom is the snake's saliva, or spit. It is made in parts called venom, or salivary, glands. There is one under each eye. The venom is delivered by two fangs in the upper jaw. When the snake bites into prey, the venom is squeezed along or through the fangs, into the victim.

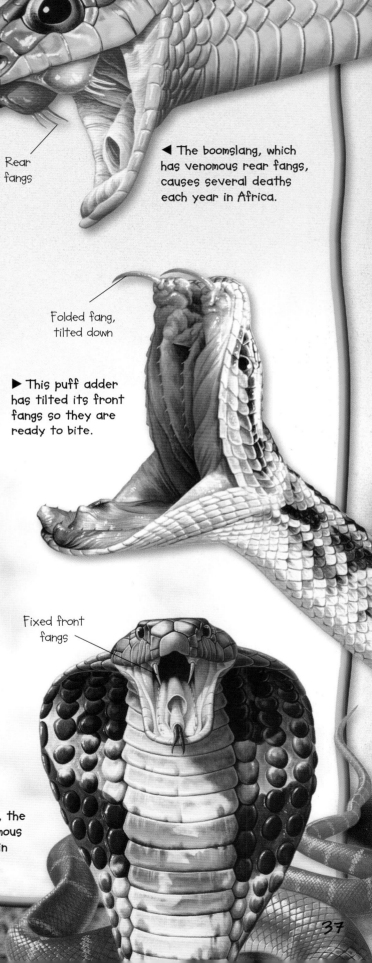

74 Rear-fanged snakes deliver their venom with long teeth at the back of their mouths. Cat-eyed, hooknose and lyre snakes are all rear-fanged snakes. More dangerous are twig and vine snakes, and most deadly of all is the boomslang. These snakes hold victims in their mouths and 'chew' so the fangs inject venom deep into the wound.

Rear fangs

◄ The boomslang, which has venomous rear fangs, causes several deaths each year in Africa.

75 Other snakes deliver venom with fangs at the front of the mouth, so they can strike fast then retreat as the victim dies. Some snakes such as night adders, puff adders, rattlesnakes, lanceheads and pit vipers have folded fangs that lay against the upper jaw bone, but can swivel or tilt so they are pointing downwards. As they strike, they jab in venom deeply.

Folded fang, tilted down

► This puff adder has tilted its front fangs so they are ready to bite.

76 Not all front-fanged snakes have folded fangs — instead some have fixed teeth that don't move. One group of fixed front-fanged snakes are the elapids. This group includes coral snakes, cobras, mambas, adders, kraits and sea snakes. Their fangs have grooves or tubes to deliver venom.

Fixed front fangs

► At more than 5 metres long, the king cobra is the biggest venomous snake. Fast and fierce, its main prey is other snakes.

37

Lethal lizards

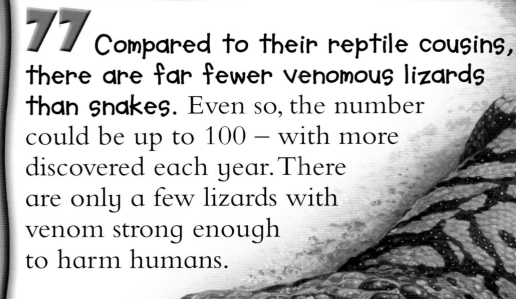

77 Compared to their reptile cousins, there are far fewer venomous lizards than snakes. Even so, the number could be up to 100 – with more discovered each year. There are only a few lizards with venom strong enough to harm humans.

Venom gland

Sharp, grooved teeth

▲ Gila monsters grow to 60 centimetres in length and are stocky, powerful lizards. They live in dry scrub and desert habitats (homes).

78 Two well known venomous lizards are the gila monster and the beaded lizard, of North and Central America. Like snakes, their venom is a type of saliva. These two lizards produce venom in glands in the lower jaw (unlike snakes, which have glands in the upper jaw).

79 The gila monster and beaded lizard are closely related and use their venom in similar ways. Each lizard bites its prey and chews. The venom oozes along its jaws and teeth into the victim. These lizards can bite very hard for a long time. The venom causes great pain and swelling but it is not deadly to humans.

I DON'T BELIEVE IT!

If a gila monster lizard bites, it usually hangs on so hard that the only way to loosen its grip is to put the whole lizard underwater.

During defense displays, the lizard extends its 'beard'

Sharp spines on the throat

▲ Bearded dragon lizards have tiny glands along both the upper and lower jaws that may produce a weak venom.

80 It was recently discovered that the world's biggest lizard, the Komodo dragon, may have a venomous bite. For a long time scientists thought that the lizard's victims died quickly from germs seeping into wounds made by its bites. But a substance found in its saliva could possibly be a venom – experts are still investigating.

81 The Komodo dragon is a type of monitor lizard. Other monitors are also being studied to see if they have venomous bites – as are some other lizards, such as iguanas and legless lizards.

▶ Three-metre-long Komodo dragons are expert predators. They often wound prey with a vicious bite before stalking it and waiting for it to weaken.

Mammal bites and spurs

82 Of all the animal groups, mammals have the fewest venomous creatures. Most venomous mammals don't have venom strong enough to do much harm to people, apart from one kind – the duck-billed platypus of Australia.

Venomous spur

83 It is not known for definite why there are so few venomous mammals. Perhaps other animal groups, such as reptiles, evolved (developed) venom millions of years ago. Then new kinds of animals evolved from these original ancestors, and kept the ability to make venom. Venomous mammals evolved venom relatively recently.

84 Several kinds of shrews have venomous bites. They use the venom to disable and paralyze prey by biting hard and chewing with great speed. This is useful because shrews are very small, and often their prey is bigger and stronger than they are.

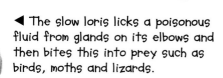

◀ The slow loris licks a poisonous fluid from glands on its elbows and then bites this into prey such as birds, moths and lizards.

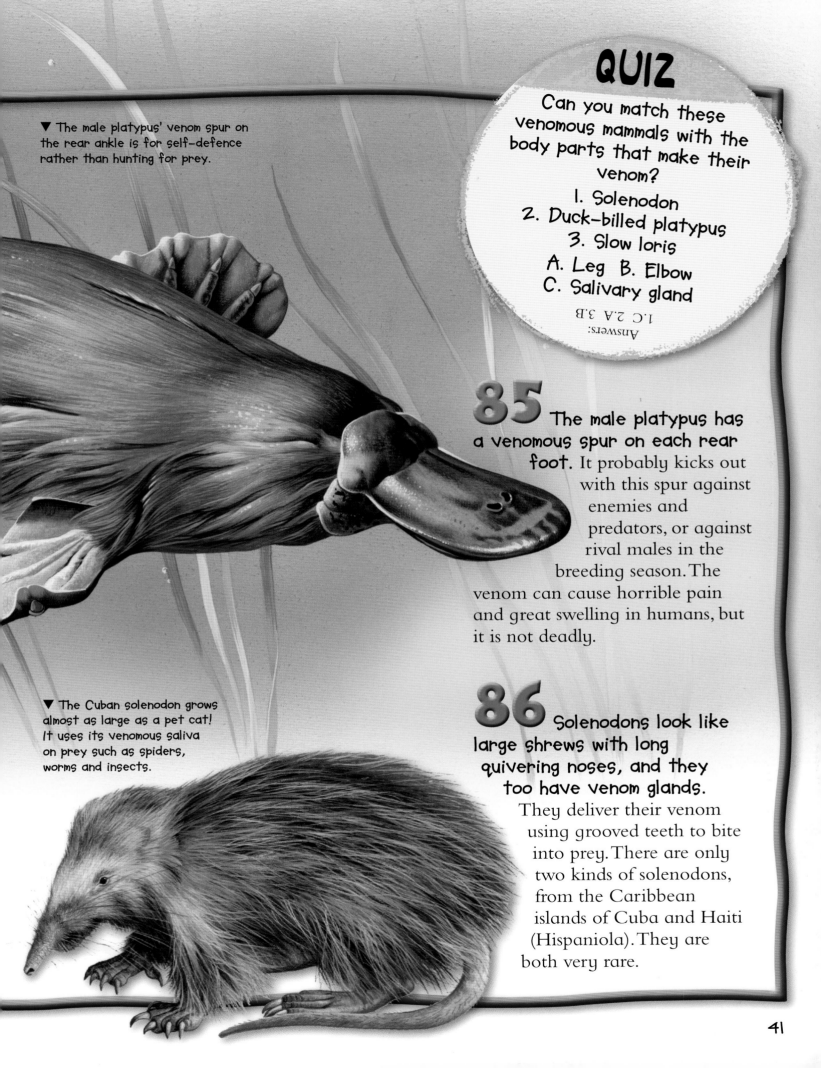

▼ The male platypus' venom spur on the rear ankle is for self-defence rather than hunting for prey.

85 **The male platypus has a venomous spur on each rear foot.** It probably kicks out with this spur against enemies and predators, or against rival males in the breeding season. The venom can cause horrible pain and great swelling in humans, but it is not deadly.

▼ The Cuban solenodon grows almost as large as a pet cat! It uses its venomous saliva on prey such as spiders, worms and insects.

86 **Solenodons look like large shrews with long quivering noses, and they too have venom glands.** They deliver their venom using grooved teeth to bite into prey. There are only two kinds of solenodons, from the Caribbean islands of Cuba and Haiti (Hispaniola). They are both very rare.

Friends and enemies

87 **Most venomous animals wander and hunt alone.** But a few live in groups and help each other to catch prey and defend themselves. Social huntsman spiders live in groups of around 100. They gang up to attack large prey.

88 **Many sea anemones allow certain sea creatures to live among their stinging tentacles.** Clownfish have a special slimy body covering and also a bodily resistance, or immunity, to their anemone's venom. Some kinds of shrimps or prawns are protected by the anemone's tentacles, and in return they eat bits of leftover food to keep the anemone clean.

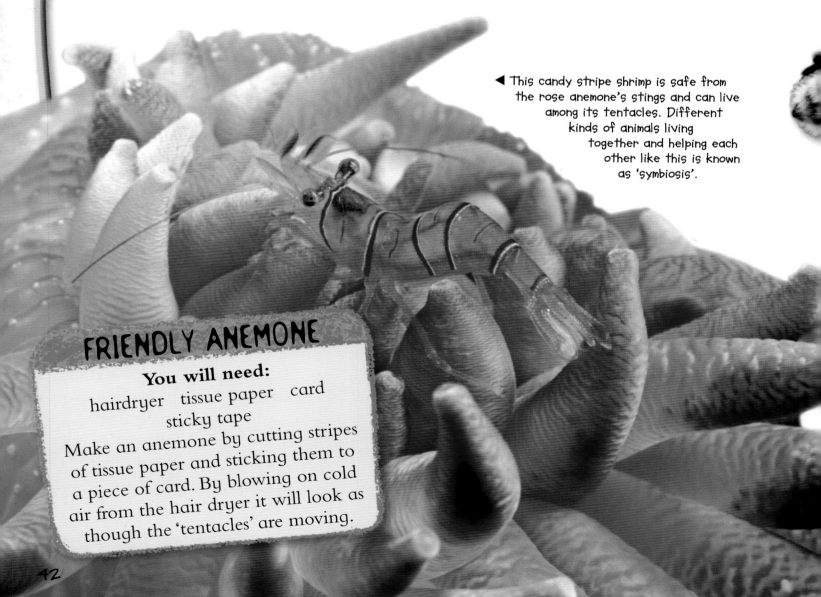

◄ This candy stripe shrimp is safe from the rose anemone's stings and can live among its tentacles. Different kinds of animals living together and helping each other like this is known as 'symbiosis'.

FRIENDLY ANEMONE

You will need:
hairdryer   tissue paper   card
sticky tape
Make an anemone by cutting stripes of tissue paper and sticking them to a piece of card. By blowing on cold air from the hair dryer it will look as though the 'tentacles' are moving.

▶ The bonnethead, a type of hammerhead shark, can eat stingrays without suffering effects of the venom.

89 Some predators are resistant or immune to venom, even if it does get into their bodies. This is due to their body chemistry, which breaks down the venom quickly before it can do damage. Hammerhead sharks eat stingrays and even swallow their venomous spines, while kingsnakes are immune to rattlesnake venom – they attack and swallow them.

90 Even very venomous animals have enemies that attack and kill them for food. The mongoose and secretary bird kill and eat venomous snakes, and bee-eater birds catch bees and wasps. Usually the attacker has enough speed and skill to avoid being bitten or stung, as well as thick skin and fur or feathers for protection.

▶ The secretary bird relies on speed, agility and tough scales on its legs for protection as it stamps on venomous snakes to eat.

▶ The bee-eater bird holds its victim carefully in its hard beak and then rubs or bashes it on a branch or rock to get rid of the sting.

Most deadly

91 **People are fascinated with venomous animals, and want to know which is the deadliest.** But gathering serious scientific evidence to prove this is difficult and complicated. Experts continually make new discoveries about venomous animals, which change the 'most venomous' lists.

92 **Some lists put together are from people who have been bitten or stung.** But a snake or spider, for example, can bite and be gone in just a second. It is often very difficult to identify exactly which kind is responsible.

◀ Box jellyfish venom attacks the skin, nerves and heart within minutes. They have up to 60 tentacles, which can be over 3 metres long, and each has as many as 5000 stingers!

WANTED

WANTED

▶ One of the most venomous animals, the stonefish of Southeast Asia and Australia is also one of the best camouflaged.

93 Other 'most venomous' lists are based on information recorded from real-life incidents. This takes into account how aggressive venomous animals are and how much venom they deliver in real-life situations. One problem with using this method is that some deaths are not reported, especially in remote areas.

▼ The death stalker scorpion has weak pincers and relies on its venom to kill prey.

WANTED

▼ Australia's inland taipan, almost 3 metres long, has the strongest venom of any snake – 200 times more powerful than that of a rattlesnake.

94 Most venomous lists can also be affected by whether treatment exists. Before the 1980s, many people died from the bites of Sydney funnel-web spiders. Since the anti-venom was produced, there have been no known deaths, despite more bites reported. The funnel-web spider itself is just as venomous, and still bites people but it kills no one. Does the existence of an anti-venom reduce its deadliness?

95 Many lists include some of the same animals. The box jellyfish, Brazilian wandering spider, death stalker scorpion, blue-ringed octopus, stonefish, Asian cobra, Russell's viper and inland taipan are all often contenders in most deadly venomous creature line-ups.

WANTED

Valuable venom

96 Scientists are discovering the incredible medical potential of venom. One example is bee venom – it may have anti-inflammatory substances, which can reduce swelling and pain. This method seems to work in some cases, but it's difficult to ensure the good effects whilst avoiding the bad, such as pain, swelling or allergic reactions.

▲ Sydney funnel-web spiders can be tricked into oozing drops of venom from their fangs, which is then sucked up by a narrow glass tube.

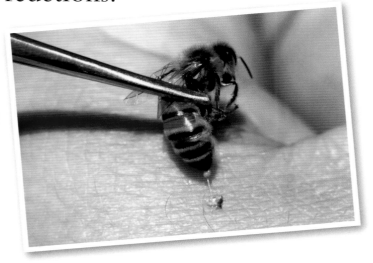

▲ People are checked to make sure they are not allergic to bee venom, before using it as possible treatment.

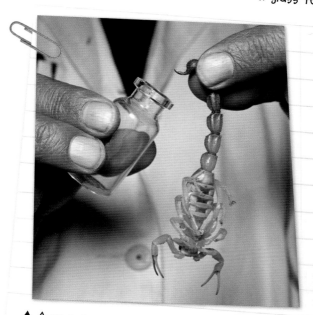

▲ A scorpion is milked by stroking and massaging the tail end so its venom sprays or drips into a glass flask.

97 An anti-venom is a substance that works against a particular venom to reduce its harm. To develop anti-venoms, first the venom itself is obtained in pure form so scientists can study it. This is done by 'milking' the animal, making them eject their venom or by taking samples from dead animals.

▲ To milk a snake, it is encouraged to bite though a plastic sheet over a container so its venom seeps out.

99 Some venomous animals are kept as pets. It's a dangerous hobby but keepers can help by studying the animals, their habits and how they behave. In turn, this helps conservation of rare venomous animals.

98 Studying venoms can lead to useful medicines and drugs. Scientists are testing substances in snake venom to treat strokes and some forms of cancers. Coneshell venom is being tested for many medical uses including painkilling drugs.

▼ Coneshells are kept in glass tanks of seawater so their venom can be collected when needed.

100 Through scientific research we can learn more about venomous animals. Discovering how and why animals use venom will allow us to reduce human suffering and protect the animals themselves, which are often killed. With more knowledge, hopefully fewer people will put themselves at risk, and venomous animals can exist without being feared or misunderstood.

Index

Entries in **bold** refer to main subject entries; entries in *italics* refer to illustrations.